by Linda Roach

HOUGHTON MIFFLIN BOSTON

Skin cells

Your Body's Building Blocks

Did you ever look closely at the palm of your hand? Take a look now. Do you know what your skin is made of? Millions of cells make up the skin that you see.

You can't see your skin cells. They are too small. All human body cells are very small. You could put about 10,000 of them on the top of a little metal pin. That's why people use microscopes to see most cells. A microscope is a tool that makes small things look bigger.

Your skin is made up of cells. Cells make up all parts of your body. Cells are the building blocks of the body. Your body has trillions of cells.

The cells shown in the pictures on these pages are just a few of the many kinds of cells in your body. Why do your body cells have so many different shapes? Each kind of cell has a different job. The different shapes help each cell do its job.

Look at the shape of the nerve cell. It has many long, thin branches. These branches help the nerve cell send out and get back nerve messages. They connect the nerve cell with many other nerve cells.

The red blood cell has a very different shape. It must go through tiny blood vessels throughout your body. Its rounded shape helps the blood cell move easily through the vessels.

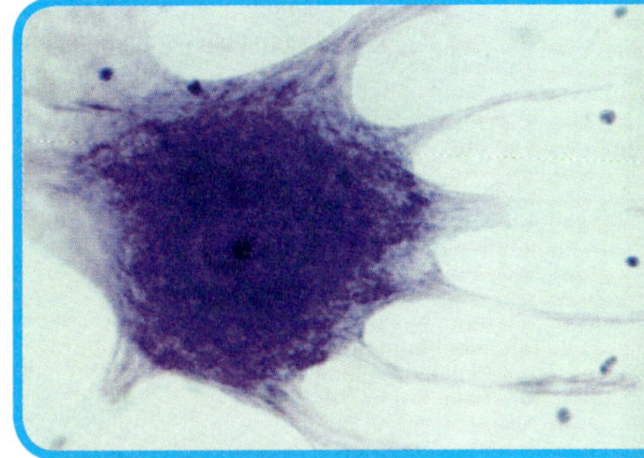

Nerve cell

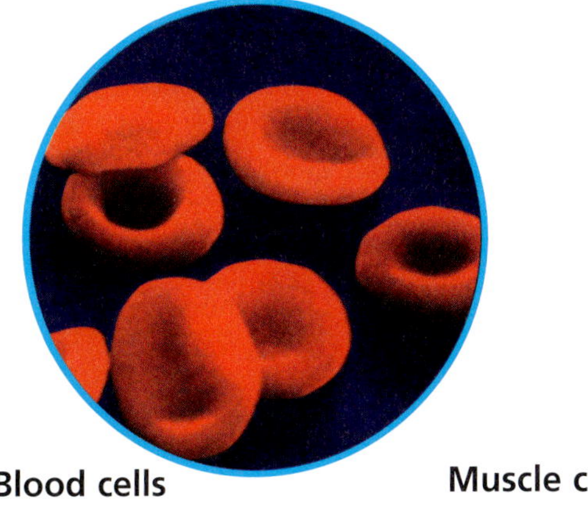

Blood cells

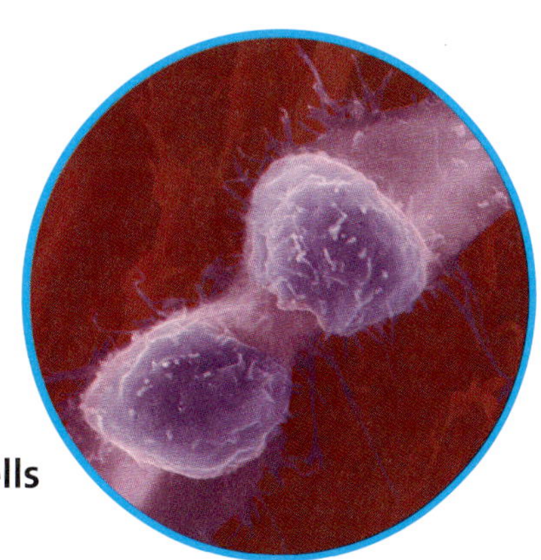

Muscle cells

Looking Inside Cells

The cells in your body have different shapes and jobs. But all cells have some of the same parts. The smaller parts in a cell are called organelles. Your skin cells have some of the same organelles found in the cells of all other living things.

Look at the picture of the animal cell below. It shows some organelles. Find the name of each organelle. Read about what each organelle does.

The organelles of an animal cell

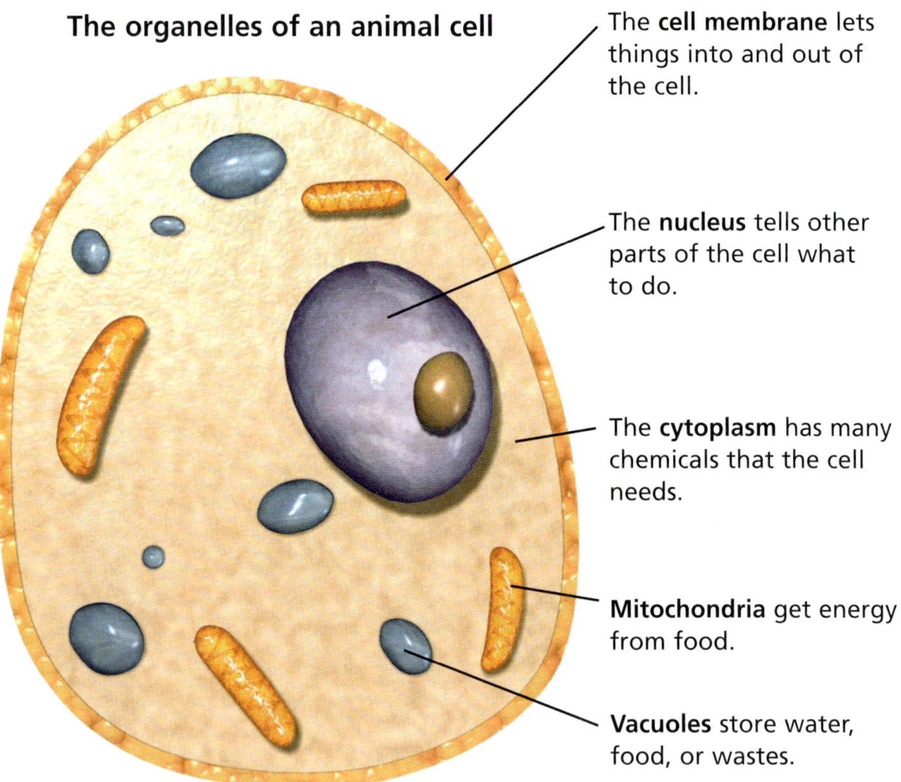

The organelles of a plant cell

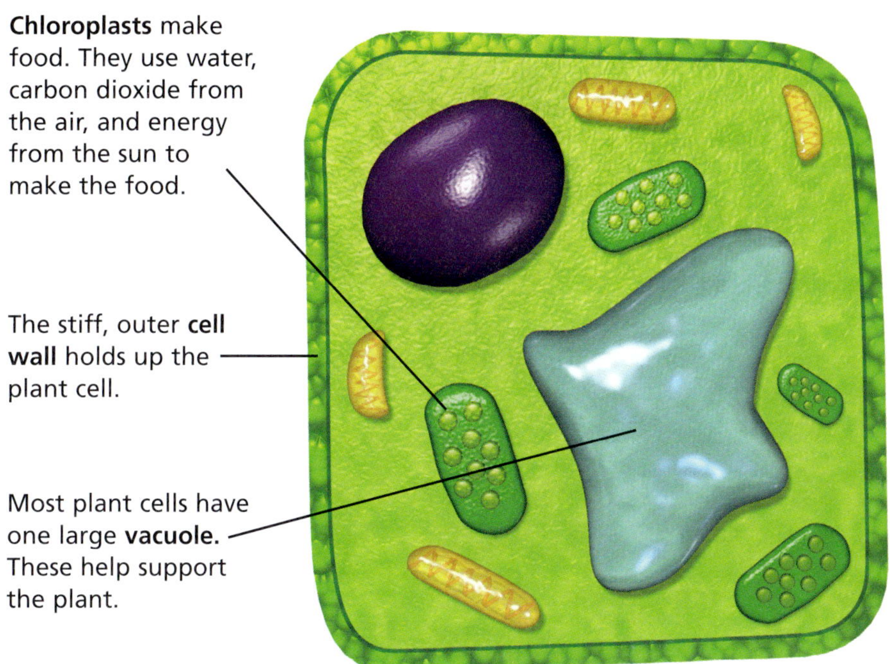

Plant Cells

The picture above is a plant cell. Compare it to the animal cell on page 4. Some of the organelles in plant cells are not found in animal cells. Most plant cells have special organelles.

The cell membrane keeps out materials that might harm the cell.

Moving Materials In and Out

The cell is like a factory where things are made. It is a busy place. Something is happening every minute of the day. What goes on inside a cell all day?

A factory needs materials to do its work. Your body's cells also need materials to do their work. Cells need food, water, and oxygen. How does a cell get the things it needs? The food, water, and oxygen enter the cell through the cell membrane. The cell membrane lets some materials into the cell. But it keeps harmful materials out.

The cell membrane also controls what leaves the cell. It lets wastes pass out of the cell. But it keeps materials the cell needs inside the cell.

What causes materials to move in and out of a cell? A process called diffusion makes many little things called particles move. Look at the picture of diffusion below. It shows how particles move. They move from an area where there are more particles to an area where there are fewer particles.

For example, blood carries food to all your body cells. The blood has many food particles. They move from the blood to your cells because your cells have less food particles. Your cells need food all the time, so this process never ends.

Your cells also produce wastes. These wastes must be removed from the cell, or the cell will die. Many wastes leave a cell by diffusion.

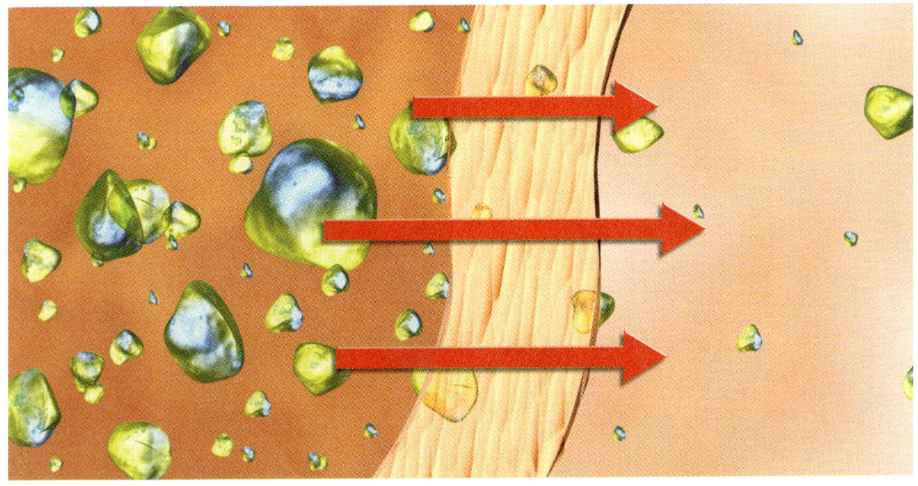

Fewer food particles are inside the cell than outside. Food particles move through the cell membrane by diffusion.

Releasing Energy

A cell is always busy. It moves materials around inside the cell. It makes sure all cell parts get the materials they need. The cell also grows. It fixes cell parts that are not working right. Some cells divide in half to form two new cells.

A cell needs energy to do all these things. Your cells get the energy they need from the food you eat. However, apples and oranges cannot fit into your cells. They are much too big. So how does the energy get into your cells?

As you eat, your body breaks down food from big pieces to littler and littler ones. It changes the food into a form that your cells can use. The food is in the form of sugar. The sugar that goes into a cell has energy. The cell gets the energy out of the sugar.

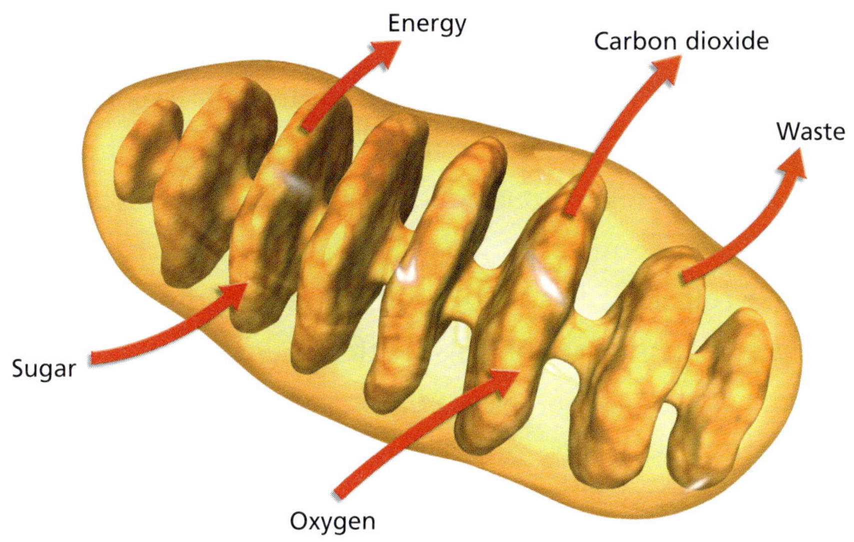

A cell's mitochondria gets the energy from the sugar. Cells use a gas called oxygen to break down the sugar. The sugar is broken down into water and another gas called carbon dioxide. That makes energy.

The carbon dioxide that is made when sugar breaks down is a waste. If too much waste is in a cell, the cell could die. The carbon dioxide that is made when sugar breaks down moves out of the cell and into your blood by diffusion.

Right now all your cells are breaking down sugar. With so many cells, your body needs a lot of sugar and oxygen. That is why you breathe. When you breathe in, you take in the oxygen your cells need. You let carbon dioxide out of your body when you breathe out.

A Group Project

A big job is hard to do alone. You can do it easier with a group of people. Think about it. Washing a car without any help would take a long time. If some friends helped, you could do the job much faster.

Your cells have big jobs, too. Often these jobs can be done better by a group of cells. Different groups of cells do different jobs. A group of cells of the same kind that work together to do a job are called a tissue.

The job of muscles is to move bones. One muscle cell cannot move a bone. But a group of muscle cells can work together to move a bone. A group of muscle cells make a muscle tissue.

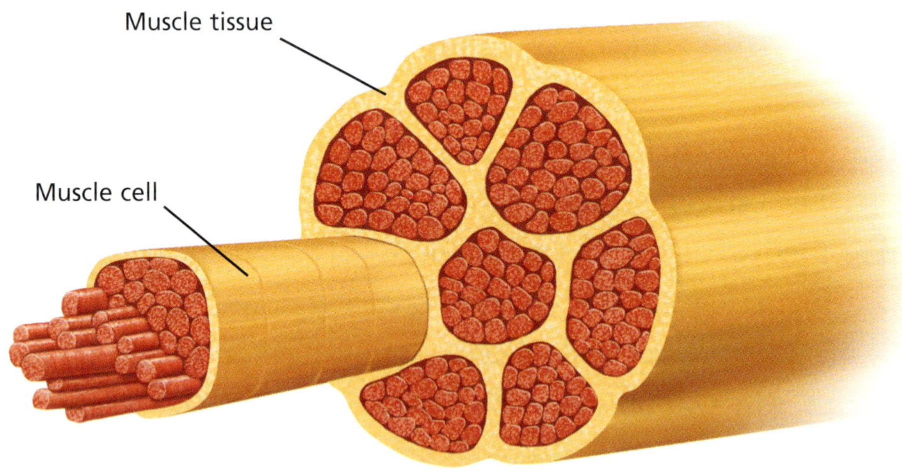

Muscles cells are long and thin. To move bones, the cells make themselves shorter. Messages from nerve tissue tell the cells to become shorter. Other tissues also help muscle tissue move bones. Together these tissues form a muscle.

A group of tissues working together to do a job are called an organ. For example, your heart is an organ that pumps blood throughout your body. A muscle is also an organ.

The organs in your body are grouped into body systems. You may have heard of some of these systems. The muscular system is made up of muscles. The digestive system is made up of the organs that break down food. The organs in body systems work together. They carry out important processes that keep you alive.

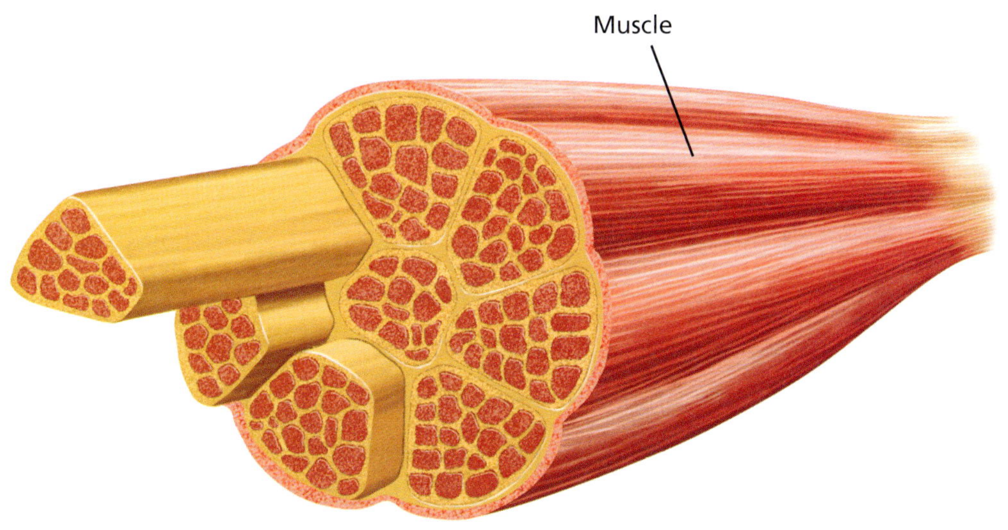

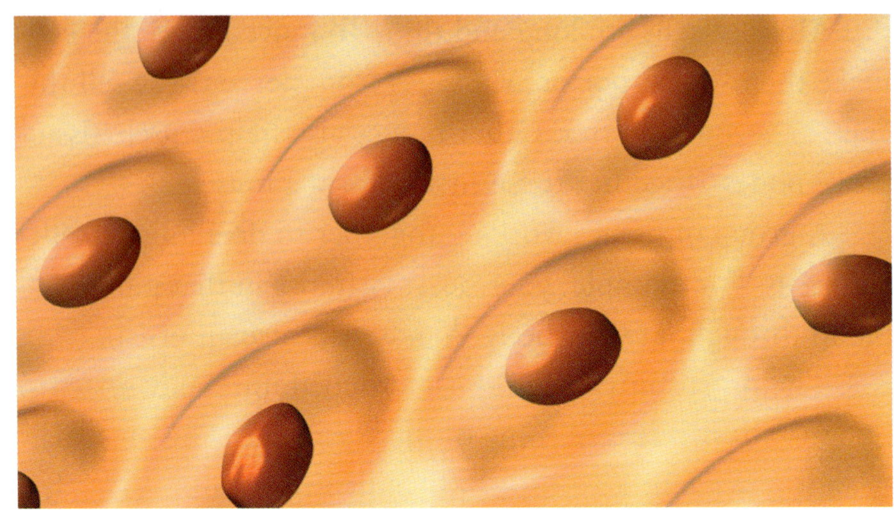

A Skin Cell's Story

Here is the story of one cell. It can help you understand what a cell's life is like.

I'm a skin cell, and I don't live alone. I live in your body's largest organ, which is the skin. I'm just one small part of the skin.

You can see in the picture that the skin is made of many layers. Find the bottom layer of the outer part of the skin. That is where I started my life. Cells grow and divide there to form new skin cells.

Today, I have finally become a grown-up cell. I'm ready to move to the top layer of the skin. I won't get all the way to the top today. The trip will take at least two weeks. It may even take a month!

I'll be busy during my trip to the top layer of the skin. Materials will move in, around, and out of me all the time. My mitochondria will work hard to release energy so that I can stay healthy.

When I get to the top of the skin, I will take the place of older cells that have died. The part of the skin you see on your hands and every other part of your body is made of dead skin cells. Dead cells rub off your skin all the time. You may lose about 10 pounds (4.4 kilograms) of dead cells in a year. Don't worry! Your skin won't wear out. Special skin cells work all the time to make more skin cells like me.

In a few weeks, I will rub off your skin. My life is short. But I'll know that I've done an important job. I help protect your body by keeping out germs and keeping in water.

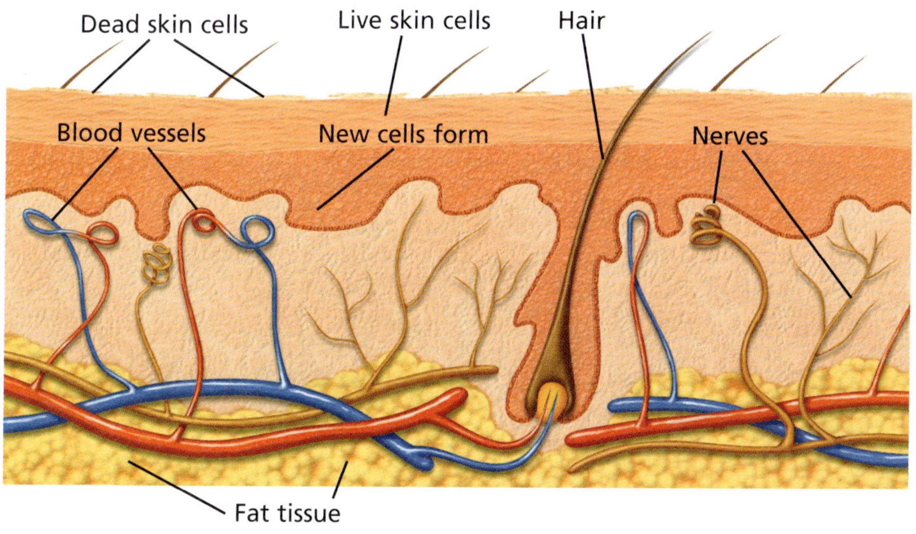

What do you know about your body's cells?

Blood

- About 8 million blood cells in the body die every minute.
- About 5 million red blood cells are in one drop of blood.
- Red blood cells live for about four months.

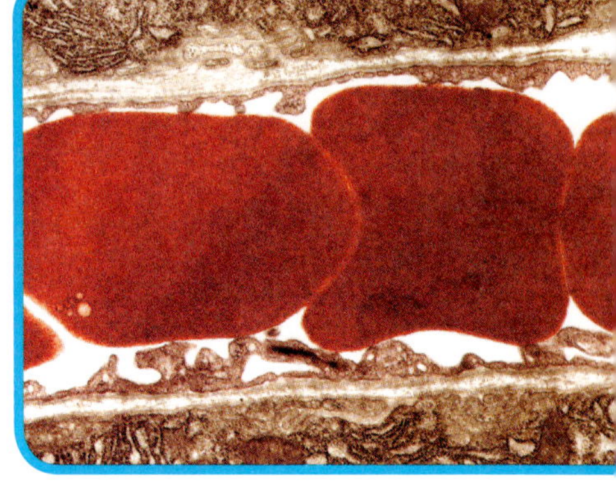

Red blood cells

Skin

- The skin is the largest organ in the body! If you spread out your skin, it would be about the size of a blanket on a child's bed.
- A piece of skin that measures one inch on each side has about 1,300 nerve cells, 3 million skin cells, and 3.2 yards (3 meters) of blood vessels.

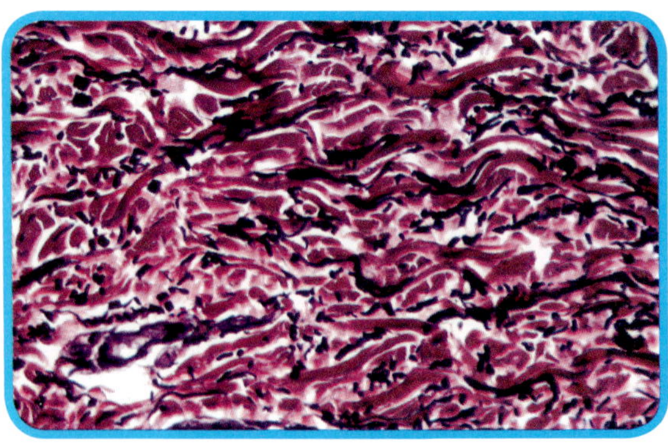

Skin tissue

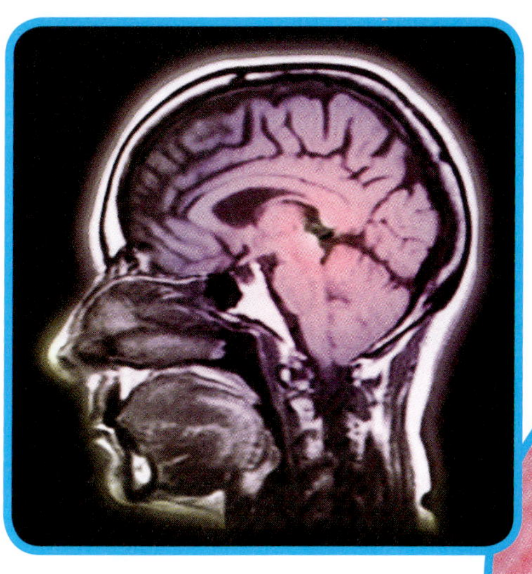

Brain

Muscle tissue

Nerves

- An adult has about 13,500,000 nerve cells in the spinal cord.
- The human brain has about 100 billion nerve cells.
- Nerve messages travel as fast as 268 miles per hour (429 kilometers/hour).

Muscles

- Muscle cells are about as thick as the hair on your head.
- Muscle cells can be as long as a muscle.
- Each cell has hundreds of parts that allow the cell to get shorter.

Activity

Plant and Animal Cells

Materials Needed

microscope
prepared slide of an onion cell
prepared slide of a skin cell

What to Do

1. Put the slide of the skin cell on the stage of the microscope.
2. Turn the adjustment knob of the microscope to bring the lens close to the slide. The lens should not touch the slide.
3. Look through the eyepiece to find the skin cell. Turn the adjustment knob until you can see the cell clearly.
4. Draw what you see. Label the nucleus, cytoplasm, and cell membrane.
5. Remove the slide. Repeat steps 1 through 4 with the onion cell.

What Did You See?

How are the cells alike? How are they different?